The Loudest

RANDOM HOUSE 🏠 NEW YORK

Address: North America, Europe, and Asia

Size: Height at shoulders: about 2 to 3 feet; length (including tail): from 4 to 6.5 feet

Weight: From 60 to 175 pounds

Favorite food: Large mammals, such as deer, elk, caribou, and sheep

The Gray Wolf

No need for cell phones here! Gray wolves communicate long-distance by howling. . . .

Gray wolves like the company of other wolves. They live in packs of mostly family members, and the strongest male is usually the leader. To communicate, they use different sounds: moans to express their unhappiness, barks and growls to challenge each other, and howls to keep the pack together.

With evening howls, they call each other to gather for the hunt. Morning howls announce their return to the pack. When danger is near, gray wolves howl an SOS. With their keen sense of hearing, they can hear a cry of distress from almost 4 miles away!

The howl of one gray wolf lasts only about 5 seconds, but others in the pack often take it up. These group, or "communal," howls can rise and fall in pitch or break off suddenly. They continue until the animals get tired or wander away. The sound of their chorus can range from sad to happy to haunting.

Address: India and Sri Lanka

Size: Male: About 7 feet high (including tail)
Female: About 3 feet high

Weight: From 4.5 to 11 pounds

Favorite food: Buds, seeds, grains, and insects

The Indian Peafowl

When it bugles in its high-pitched voice, the male Indian peafowl spreads its tail feathers to form a giant fan— fit for a fashion show!

Living in the wild, this cousin of the guinea fowl and pheasant is constantly on the lookout. Danger is never far in the tropical forests where it lives. Leopards and tigers eat peafowl for dinner! At the slightest sound, the peafowl trumpets an alarm that echoes for almost a mile.

The Indian peafowl generally flies only when it is in danger. If frightened, it will noisily flap its wings and rise into the treetops.

Peafowl are creatures of habit. They sleep roosted in the same tree and trumpet at the same time every day, as if part of a ritual.

During courtship, the male peafowl (called a peacock) shrieks, "lee-YOW, lee-YOW, lee-YOW." Then, with great showmanship, he spreads his magnificent blue-green tail feathers into a fan and performs a mating dance.

The female, or peahen (whose feathers are grayish and who has no fan), easily falls under the charm of the male— and who can blame her? Besides being good-looking, he's a talented singer and dancer!

Address: Africa and northwestern India

Size: From 8 to 11 feet long (including tail)

Weight: From 265 to 525 pounds

Favorite food: Zebra, cape buffalo, and antelope

The Lion

When a lion roars, it makes so much noise that the ground vibrates under its paws!

Standing with its head tilted toward the ground and its sides taut, the lion expands its chest like a balloon. Then the king of beasts opens its mouth and lets out a roar so powerful . . . it can kick up clouds of dust! In the savanna, the sound can be heard for a distance of over 5 miles. The lion marks off its territory: all who hear its roar know that the best way to avoid trouble is to retreat. In the savanna, the lion is one scary animal. But the lion rarely looks for a fight. It prefers to use its intimidating voice to make itself understood.

This giant feline lives in groups—called prides—of typically 5 to 10 females and their young and 2 or 3 males. Under the protection of the males (who watch from a distance), the lionesses hunt zebra, cape buffalo, gnu, gazelle, and other antelope. They are followed into the hunt by their cubs. The roars of these young hunters sound like the mewing of big house cats with colds.

After the female kills the prey, His Majesty King Lion pushes her aside so he can eat first. In a single meal, an adult male lion can devour some 65 to 90 pounds of meat.

At dawn, the lion opens its mouth wide and yawns so hard, it seems as if its jaws will dislocate! With a full stomach, it roars loudly with contentment before taking a nap for 20 hours or so in the shade of the acacia trees.

To croak twice as loudly as usual, the male edible frog inflates a sac on his neck, like a big bubble of gum.

The Edible Frog

Europe

Address: Europe

Size: From 2 to 6 inches long

Favorite food: Insects, other frogs, and fish

Come spring, edible frogs really make a racket! The males are equipped with inflatable sacs on each side of their mouths that amplify, or make louder, their croaks. Their mating call—which is like a banjo being plucked—can be heard over a quarter of a mile away! These moonlit concerts by the water's edge can last for hours.

Mating season is also the time for the edible frog to stock up on food. To eat, they catch insects by trapping them with their long, sticky tongues. One edible frog can swallow up to 100 insects a day! But because they are so often busy singing, eating, or mating, the edible frogs often get eaten themselves—by wading birds, fish, turtles, snakes, and raccoons.

Female edible frogs lay hundreds of tiny, round, jelly-like eggs that float on the water. When the babies hatch from the eggs, they are called tadpoles. Depending on the temperature, they can take from 3 to 22 months to transform into frogs.

Over the winter, edible frogs bury themselves in the bottom of ponds to keep from freezing. There, they stay silent . . . until spring, when their croaking chorus starts again.

Address: North America, Europe, and Asia

Size: From 4 to 5.5 feet at the shoulders

Weight: Male: From 330 to 550 pounds
Female: About 220 pounds

Favorite food: Vegetation and bark

The Red Deer

To intimidate its rivals and attract does, the male red deer makes a sound somewhere between a cow's moo and a lion's roar. . . .

Come October, the red deer is raring to start roaring! It's courting season, and the stags are in fierce competition for the females' attentions.

Before doing battle, the stags gallop through the woods bellowing fiercely. At dusk, the territorial male lets out deep, powerful roars. He bangs the antlers crowning his head against tree branches, in training for the big fight.

Then the combat begins. Face to face, the stags violently paw the ground with their hooves. Gnashing their teeth, they drive into one another head-on and lock their great antlers, which can weigh 30 to 35 pounds.

The winner of this fight may reign over as many as 20 does. After mating with each of them, the stag goes off for a quiet rest deep in the forest. His antlers fall off in February. But by the end of summer, they will have grown back, and the stag may bellow once again, confident he will conquer his rivals.

The Black-

This squealing European seabird vacations at American beaches. . . .

Black-headed gulls are identified by their brick-red bill and legs—and their harsh voice. *Kree-ah! Kree-ah!*

They are the most common gulls found in Europe and are regular winter visitors to eastern North America. They live in noisy colonies of hundreds, even thousands, of birds, located on sand dunes, beaches, marshes, and open fields. In the summer—when they breed—their heads take on a hood of dark brown feathers. During the winter—when they visit us—their heads turn white.

More than any other gulls, black-headed gulls feed on small land animals, including hedgehogs and other potential egg and/or chick robbers. They also eat fish and will pursue dragonflies and other flying insects, along with a variety of other invertebrates.

While visiting the USA, black-headed gulls tend to keep company with the native gulls. What a bunch of loudmouths!

Address: Eastern North America and Europe

Size: About 15 inches long

Weight: From 7 to 9 ounces

Favorite food: Worms, fish, shellfish, and whatever it can scavenge

Europe

North America

Headed Gull

Address: Central and South America

Size: Up to 31 inches long, plus a 31-inch-long tail

Weight: From 8 to 22 pounds

Favorite food: Buds, leaves, flowers, and fruit

The Howler Monkey

The noisiest of all monkeys makes such a loud sound, he sometimes scares off the most dangerous of predators!

The cries of the howler monkey are best heard at dawn and dusk. The strongest male of each clan slowly begins to warm up his voice, like an opera singer practicing scales. Only these scales sound like the engine of a car being started! Like the bag on a set of bagpipes, the howler monkey's vocal sac (located in the center of his throat) begins to inflate.

The leader of the clan lets out a long, low cry, which can last between 3 and 5 minutes. Very quickly, the other monkeys in the group begin to imitate him. Their cries can turn into an ear-splitting concert—heard some 1 to 2.5 miles through the jungle!

After establishing the clan's territory, the leader makes a funny gurgling sound, like an emptying drain. He is expelling all the extra air in his vocal sac.

If the male howler monkey senses danger during the day, it makes a series of short, quick, muted sounds, warning the female members of the clan to stay with the babies. But whatever happens, the howler monkeys are real "family types" who never stray very far from one another. So, unlike other monkeys, they don't have to spend all day screeching to each other to indicate their location.

The Great Spotted Woodpecker

Rat-a-tat-tat-tat-tat-tat-tat!
The great spotted woodpecker batters tree trunks 10 to 12 times a second, like a miniature sledgehammer. . . .

In the springtime, the noisiest of the forest birds chooses a tree to peck that will make the best sound, ideally a dry branch or hollow tree trunk. Then, to attract the attention of his sweetheart, the male great spotted woodpecker hammers the bark with all his might. His thousands of beak taps can be heard half a mile away. *Rat-a-tat-tat-tat-tat-tat-tat!* The female answers him by hammering back.

With its quick, sharp taps, the great spotted woodpecker marks off its territory and loosens the tree bark to capture bugs hidden underneath.

With all that banging, the great spotted woodpecker's beak suffers a lot of wear and tear. Fortunately, its beak does not wear out: it constantly grows to combat the wear!

Woodpeckers also use their beak to dig nests in tree cavities. The female lays from 4 to 7 eggs there each year. In the nest, baby woodpeckers can be heard crying, "*keek, keek, keek . . . ,*" which means they are demanding to be fed. Their parents have to unroll their sticky tongues and feed the little squealers over 150 times a day!

Europe

North Africa

Asia

Address: Europe, North Africa, and Asia
Size: About 10 inches long
Weight: About 2.5 ounces
Favorite food: Insects, conifer seeds, eggs, some fruit, and occasionally baby birds

Africa

Address: The southern Sahara in Africa

Size: About 5 feet long, plus a 10-inch-long tail

Weight: 88 to 175 pounds (Females are up to 14% heavier than males.)

Favorite food: Zebra, antelope, and carrion

The Spotted Hyena

With a huge burst of laughter, the hyena invites its gang to feast on fresh meat. . . .

The hyena is no loner. It lives in a noisy clan of 10 to over 50 animals, which is led by the strongest female in the group. Each evening, the spotted hyenas take off for the hunt, making sounds like very high, piercing laughs. In the savanna, this laughing can be heard almost 2 miles away. Once they spot their prey, the hungry hyenas run as fast as 30 miles per hour.

Then suddenly, they begin to laugh louder and louder to show their glee. There'll be plenty of dinner tonight: their prey—a gnu—is too sick to defend itself.

When they laugh, hyenas reveal their powerful jaws. Their premolars can break horn and bone like nutcrackers. Because they are noisy eaters, hyenas attract the attention of other wild animals. Then it may be their turn to be hunted and feasted upon. But not always. By screaming furiously, hyenas can intimidate a lion, sometimes even stealing its meal!

When dawn breaks, the hyenas go back to their den. There they sleep and rest their vocal cords until night falls.

Address: Europe, Africa, and Asia

Size: From 3 to 4.5 feet high at the shoulders

Weight: About 325 pounds

Favorite food: Hay, grass, and grain

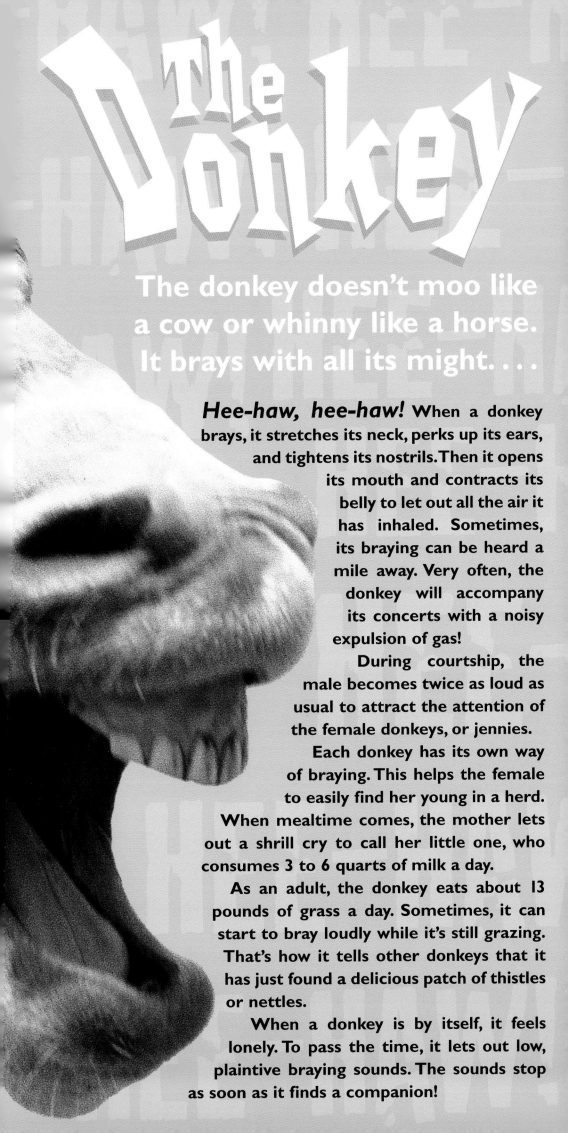

The Donkey

The donkey doesn't moo like a cow or whinny like a horse. It brays with all its might. . . .

Hee-haw, hee-haw! When a donkey brays, it stretches its neck, perks up its ears, and tightens its nostrils. Then it opens its mouth and contracts its belly to let out all the air it has inhaled. Sometimes, its braying can be heard a mile away. Very often, the donkey will accompany its concerts with a noisy expulsion of gas!

During courtship, the male becomes twice as loud as usual to attract the attention of the female donkeys, or jennies.

Each donkey has its own way of braying. This helps the female to easily find her young in a herd. When mealtime comes, the mother lets out a shrill cry to call her little one, who consumes 3 to 6 quarts of milk a day.

As an adult, the donkey eats about 13 pounds of grass a day. Sometimes, it can start to bray loudly while it's still grazing. That's how it tells other donkeys that it has just found a delicious patch of thistles or nettles.

When a donkey is by itself, it feels lonely. To pass the time, it lets out low, plaintive braying sounds. The sounds stop as soon as it finds a companion!

The American Alligator

The American alligator is the noisiest of all reptiles. Its cries are as loud as the engine of a small plane. . . .

Usually, a crocodilian wails, or, in other words, lets out weak, mournful sounds. But the American alligator roars like a lion!

The cries of the American alligator echo through the swamps: the males are trying to intimidate one another. A wild show is about to begin. They stick their short, wide snouts out of the water, displaying their sharp teeth. Bellowing loudly, they whip up their tails and violently beat the water with their jaws. Then, while blowing bubbles with their nostrils, they dive to where the females wait.

From May to July, each female American alligator can lay some 40 eggs in nests of grass and mud. The nests measure about 7 feet wide. While they are still in their eggs, the babies let out high-pitched grunts. They are telling their mothers that they will soon be hatching from their shells. Once the babies hatch, the females use their jaws like a cradle. They carefully take each of their babies into their mouths, then carry them to the water, nestled gently between their teeth. Once in the water, the baby reptiles take their first swim.

In winter, the American alligator families disappear into the muddy swamp bottom and are silent at last.

United States

Address: Southeastern United States

Size: From 8 to 16 feet long

Weight: Up to 1,100 pounds

Favorite food: Fish, frogs, snakes, and small mammals

Address: Africa

Size: From 8.5 to 11 feet high

Weight: Male: 11,000 to 13,200 pounds
Female: Up to 6,600 pounds

Favorite food: Leaves, bushes, and grasses

Africa

The African Elephant

When in danger, the grandmother elephant— who leads the herd—blows her trunk like an alarm siren!

The entire herd obeys the deafening trumpets of the oldest female elephant. The more strident, or harsh, her trumpeting, the more fear or alarm she's expressing.

If confronted by lions, the elephants charge. They stampede toward the predators at almost 25 miles per hour. In the midst of a trumpeting din, the elephants stamp the ground and spread their enormous ears like shields to make themselves appear even larger. Predators beat a hasty retreat before these massive creatures, which can measure over 10 feet high.

Once danger has passed, elephants like to bathe while trumpeting in joyful little blasts. But their trunks, which are made up of over 100,000 muscles, are not only horns. They also serve as showerheads and as giant straws for drinking up to 40 gallons of water a day.

Elephants are not just noisy when they're in danger. They also like to greet each other with a fanfare of trumpets. When two friendly clans meet, the grandmother elephants link trunks, wave their ears, and knock tusks.

The Big-Mouth Club

THE GREAT SPOTTED WOODPECKER

THE LION

THE SPOTTED HYENA

THE INDIAN PEAFOWL

THE GRAY WOLF

THE HOWLER MONKEY

THE AMERICAN ALLIGATOR

THE RED DEER

THE DONKEY

THE BLACK-HEADED GULL

THE EDIBLE FROG

THE AFRICAN ELEPHANT

Know someone
who should
join this club?
Paste his or her
picture here!

Know someone
who should
join this club?
Paste his or her
picture here!

PHOTOGRAPHS:
Gray wolf: left, Klein-Hubert/BIOS; right, Sylvain Cordier/JACANA.
Indian peafowl: cover, S. Osilinski/O.S.F./BIOS; interior left, Klein-Hubert/BIOS.
Lion: M. Nicollotti/BIOS.
Edible frog: F. Gilson/BIOS.
Red deer: C. Ruoso/BIOS.
Black-headed gull: top, G. Bortolato/BIOS; bottom, J. L. Le Moigne/BIOS.
Howler monkey: R. Walter/PHO.N.E.
Great spotted woodpecker: left, Y. Noto Campanella/BIOS; right, R. Valter/PHO.N.E.
Spotted hyena: left, C. Balcaen/BIOS; right, Y. Arthus-Bertrand/Peter Arnold/BIOS.
Donkey: H. Ausloos/BIOS.
American alligator: left, F. Labhardt/BIOS; right, H. Reinhard/OKAPIA/BIOS.
African elephant: M. and C. Denis-Huot/BIOS.

www.randomhouse.com/kids

Library of Congress Cataloging-in-Publication Data
Doinet, Mymi. The loudest / [Mymi Doinet].
   p. cm. — (Faces of nature)
ISBN 0-375-81406-X
1. Sound production by animals—Juvenile literature. [1. Animal sounds.
2. Morphology (Animals). 3. Adaptation (Biology). 4. Animals.]
I. Title. QL765 .D65 2002   591.59'4—dc21   2001019276

Printed in Malaysia February 2002   10 9 8 7 6 5 4 3 2 1
RANDOM HOUSE and colophon are registered trademarks of Random House, Inc.